RACCOONS

Meryl Magby

PowerKiDS
press

New York

Published in 2014 by The Rosen Publishing Group, Inc.
29 East 21st Street, New York, NY 10010

Copyright © 2014 by The Rosen Publishing Group, Inc.

First Edition

Editor: Amelie von Zumbusch
Book Design: Ashley Drago
Layout Design: Kate Vlachos

Photo Credits: Cover, p. 1 Stockbyte/Thinkstock; p. 3 Helen Cingisiz/Shutterstock.com; pp. 4–5, 15 (bottom), 17 iStockphoto/Thinkstock; p. 6 Becky Sheridan/Shutterstock.com; p. 7 Martha Marks/Shutterstock.com; p. 8 Fuse/Getty Images; p. 9 hadot 760/Shutterstock.com; p. 10 Bill Draker/Getty Images; p. 11 Gary Seloff/Flickr Open/Getty Images; pp. 12–13 Spiber/Shutterstock.com; p. 14 Gregory MD/Photo Researchers/Getty Images; p. 15 (top) Scott E. Read/Shutterstock.com; p. 16 J & C Sohns/Picture Press/Getty Images; p. 18 Gerald A. DeBoer/Shutterstock.com; p. 19 Heiko Kiera/Shutterstock.com; p. 20 Cornelius Krieghoff/The Bridgeman Art Library/Getty Images; p. 21 Blank Archives/Hulton Archive/Getty Images; p. 22 Jimmy Napp Photos/Shutterstock.com.

Library of Congress Cataloging-in-Publication Data

Magby, Meryl.
 Raccoons / by Meryl Magby. — 1st ed.
     p. cm. — (American animals)
 Includes index.
 ISBN 978-1-4777-0789-0 (library binding) — ISBN 978-1-4777-0950-4 (pbk.) —
 ISBN 978-1-4777-0951-1 (6-pack)
 1. Raccoon—Juvenile literature. I. Title. II. Series: Magby, Meryl. American animals.
 QL737.C26M34 2014
 599.76'32—dc23

                                              2012047623

Manufactured in the United States of America

CPSIA Compliance Information: Batch #S13PK6: For Further Information contact Rosen Publishing, New York, New York at 1-800-237-9932

Contents

Masks and Stripes

Raccoons are one of the best-known animals in the United States. This is because they live in almost every part of the country. Raccoons are easy to spot. They look like they are wearing black face masks and have bushy tails with black stripes. However, many people may have never seen a raccoon in person. This is because raccoons tend to come out at night.

There are three kinds of raccoons. The ones that live in the United States are called common raccoons. They are also known as northern raccoons.

Raccoons are **mammals**. They are native to North America and parts of South America. They belong to the same family as ringtails and white-nosed coatis. Raccoons are known for being very smart. They are also known for eating almost anything, including garbage!

From Forest to Cities

Raccoons have a very large **range** in North America. They can be found throughout the United States, except for parts of the Rocky Mountains and southwestern deserts. Raccoons also live in southern Canada and throughout Mexico.

Raccoons often live near people's homes. Some even try to move into attics or basements!

Raccoons are very **adaptable** animals. They can live in nearly any **habitat** found in the United States! Raccoons like to live in wooded areas near water, such as streams, lakes, marshes, and swamps. However, they can also be found in forests, farmland, neighborhoods, and crowded cities. Raccoons will live in almost any place where they can find food, water, and places to hide.

Raccoons need to live near water. This is why they do not live in the driest parts of deserts.

Flexible Fingers

Raccoons have round bodies that are covered in thick brown or gray fur. They have black masks on their faces and black rings on their tails. They have four black paws. Raccoon paws have five fingers, just like a person's hands do. Adults tend to weigh between 10 and 30 pounds (5–14 kg). They are about 2 to 3 feet (0.6–0.9 m) long from nose to tail.

Raccoons have an excellent sense of touch. They also hear well and have great night vision.

Raccoons are very smart and quick. They can use the **flexible** fingers on their front paws to do things that most other animals cannot do. These include untying knots and turning doorknobs!

Eating Almost Anything

Raccoons are **omnivores**. This means they eat both plants and animals. Exactly what a raccoon eats depends on where it lives. They may eat fruits, nuts, berries, seeds, eggs, insects, crayfish, frogs, fish, and turtles.

When raccoons dip their food in water, it looks like they are washing it. This is how they got their scientific name, *Procyon lotor*. It means "washing bear."

Raccoons sometimes even catch young gophers, squirrels, mice, and rats. Raccoons living near people also eat pet food and garbage.

Raccoons look for food at night. They use the many **nerves** on the bottoms of their paws to feel their food. Raccoons often dip their food in water before they eat it. Scientists think that this softens the raccoons' feet and makes it easier for them to feel their food.

Washing food in water softens the food and makes it easier for a raccoon to eat. It makes the food cleaner, too!

Raccoon Facts

2. Raccoons can remember how to solve a problem for up to three years after they were taught how to solve it.

1. Raccoon tracks are easy to recognize. Their paw prints look like small human hands!

3. A raccoon's back feet can **rotate** 180 degrees. This helps raccoons climb down trees head-first. Some other animals, such as cats, cannot do this and have to back down trees.

4. The word "raccoon" comes from *aroughcun*, which is the Powhatan people's word for the animal. *Aroughcun* means "he scratches with his hands."

5. Raccoons have flat feet, which helps them balance when they stand up on their back feet. However, it makes them waddle when they walk.

6. Raccoons make several types of noises. These include purring, snarling, snorting, growling, and a chittering sound.

7. Raccoons can swim. However, they may avoid doing so because their fur is not waterproof.

8. Raccoons can run as fast as 15 miles per hour (24 km/h)!

Night and Day

Raccoons are mostly **nocturnal**. This means that they rest during the day and are active at night. Raccoons can be pests for people in neighborhoods and cities. They tip over trash cans, dig through gardens, and pull down bird feeders looking for food. They may hide or have babies in places where they are not wanted, such as chimneys, attics, and basements.

Though people try to build bird feeders that raccoons cannot get into, raccoons are very hard to outsmart!

Raccoons keep safe from **predators** and people by hiding during the day. However, they are sometimes killed by cougars, bobcats, coyotes, dogs, owls, eagles, and snakes. They also die from hunger, being hit by cars, or getting sick.

Bobcats are about twice as big as house cats. They are fierce hunters that usually sneak up on their prey.

Like raccoons, coyotes are very adaptable. In the last 200 years, they have spread across most of North America.

15

Many Different Dens

Raccoons are thought to be solitary animals. This means adults spend most of their time alone. Raccoons tend to stay within a **home range** of about one square mile (3 sq km). In this home range, they have many hiding places that they use as dens.

Raccoons tend to stay in a den for just a few days before moving on to another one.

Raccoons eat a lot during the summer and fall. This adds more fat to their bodies, which makes it easier to live through the winter months when food is harder to find.

Unlike some other mammals, raccoons do not **hibernate** in the winter. During the winter, they spend a lot of time in their dens, keeping warm. However, they will leave their winter dens to find food if the weather is not too cold. Sometimes many raccoons will share a large den to keep warm and safe during a winter storm.

Babies and Growing Up

Raccoons **mate** in the winter. Then, the female raccoon looks for a den in which to raise her babies. In the spring, she gives birth to babies, called kits. Male raccoons do not help take care of the kits.

Kits generally leave their dens for the first time when they are about eight weeks old.

The kits' eyes stay closed for the first three weeks. At first, they drink only their mothers' milk. It helps them grow bigger and stronger. Later, the kits leave their den and follow their mother around. She teaches them how to find food and keep safe from predators and people. After about a year, the kits leave their mother to live on their own.

Newborn raccoon kits are deaf and blind. They start to see and hear within their first month.

Raccoon Hunting

Native Americans have long hunted raccoons for food and clothing. Raccoons also play a role in many Native American peoples' stories and art. Native Americans traded raccoon furs with early European settlers for tools and weapons, too.

This nineteenth-century painting shows fur traders. Fur traders helped open up the middle of North America to settlers from Europe and, later, the United States.

Settlers soon began hunting raccoons themselves. Fur trading became an important business for European settlers and explorers. Many people worked as trappers, or people who set traps to catch raccoons and other mammals. The raccoon fur was sold or traded for other goods. Raccoon pelts were often sent to Europe to be sold there. Today, many people still hunt raccoons with traps and hound dogs.

Coonskin caps were popular during the 1950s. These hats were made from raccoon skins and fur.

People and Raccoons

Raccoons are in no danger of dying out in the United States. In fact, their numbers may be growing. This may be because they have adapted so well to living in neighborhoods and cities near people.

You may see raccoons around your home at night. Raccoons can be fun to watch, but you should never get too close. Raccoons can sometimes spread diseases to people. If you like raccoons, try visiting them at a zoo or looking for their tracks in a park!

Raccoons may look cuddly, but they are wild animals. It is better not to get too close to them.

Glossary

adaptable (uh-DAP-tuh-bul) Able to change to fit requirements.

flexible (FLEK-sih-bul) Moving and bending in many ways.

habitat (HA-buh-tat) The kind of land where an animal or a plant naturally lives.

hibernate (HY-bur-nayt) To spend the winter in a sleeplike state.

home range (HOHM RAYNJ) The area in which an animal usually stays.

mammals (MA-mulz) Warm-blooded animals that have backbones and hair, breathe air, and feed milk to their young.

mate (MAYT) To come together to make babies.

nerves (NERVZ) Groups of fibers that carry messages between the brain and other parts of the body.

nocturnal (nok-TUR-nul) Active during the night.

omnivores (OM-nih-vorz) Animals that eat both plants and animals.

predators (PREH-duh-terz) Animals that kill other animals for food.

range (RAYNJ) The places in which a kind of animal can be found.

rotate (ROH-tayt) To move in a circle.

Index

Websites

Due to the changing nature of Internet links, PowerKids Press has developed an online list of websites related to the subject of this book. This site is updated regularly. Please use this link to access the list:
www.powerkidslinks.com/amer/racc/